Original title:
Northern Light

Copyright © 2024 Swan Charm
All rights reserved.

Author: Olivia Oja
ISBN HARDBACK: 978-9916-79-762-4
ISBN PAPERBACK: 978-9916-79-763-1
ISBN EBOOK: 978-9916-79-764-8

## **Radiance Through the Pines**

The sunlight dances through the leaves,
Whispers of warmth on gentle breeze.
Shadows play on the forest floor,
Nature's beauty, forevermore.

Pine needles glisten, catching light,
A tapestry of green and white.
Birds sing softly in the trees,
Echoing through the cool, sweet ease.

Branches sway with rhythmic grace,
A tranquil moment, a sacred space.
Heartbeats merge with rustling air,
In this haven, free from care.

Sunset paints the sky in hues,
Pink and gold, a vibrant muse.
As twilight falls, the stars arise,
A glimmering dance in moonlit skies.

Here I find my spirit soar,
Among the pines, forevermore.
Radiance surrounds in every phase,
In nature's arms, I lose my ways.

## Aurora's Whisper

In the stillness of night,
Soft colors take flight,
Whispers of light play,
Guiding dreams on their way.

Dancing through the skies,
A canvas that defies,
Nature's gentle brush,
In a silken hush.

Echoes of the stars,
Across the cosmos, far,
Where shadows fade thin,
And new tales begin.

In the northern glow,
The heartstrings flow,
Underneath the beams,
We chase our dreams.

As night turns to day,
In a magical way,
The aurora fades slow,
But the memories grow.

## **Celestial Dance Above**

Stars waltz in the night,
In a timeless delight,
Spinning tales of old,
In silence, they unfold.

Galaxies parade,
In a grand masquerade,
Twinkling like dreams dear,
Echoing through the sphere.

Moonlight serenades,
In soft, silver shades,
While comets ignite,
A fleeting, bright sight.

Whispers fill the air,
As constellations share,
Stories held in light,
Of love, loss, and flight.

Together they sway,
In a cosmic ballet,
The universe sings,
Of infinite things.

## Glimmering Veil of the Arctic

In the deep, frosty night,
A veil shines so bright,
Ice crystals aglow,
Where the cold winds blow.

The horizon whispers,
As the daylight shivers,
Painting skies in hues,
Of sapphire and blues.

Beneath the pale light,
The world feels so right,
With each breath of air,
A chill everywhere.

Creatures dance in white,
In the quiet twilight,
Nature's pure embrace,
In this frozen place.

As dawn starts to break,
The beauty we wake,
A landscape unreal,
In the Arctic's appeal.

## **Radiance in the Chill**

Within the winter's grasp,
A warmth we can clasp,
Fires burn bright and bold,
In the frigid cold.

Glistening snowflakes fall,
Like diamonds, they call,
In a world so serene,
Crafting magical scenes.

Echoes of laughter rise,
Underneath starlit skies,
As families unite,
In the hush of the night.

Hot cocoa in hand,
We gather and stand,
Together, we shine,
In the frosty divine.

The chill wraps around,
Yet love is profound,
In the heart's embrace,
We find our warm space.

## A Chorus of Colors Above

The sky ignites with vibrant hues,
A canvas brushed with shades anew.
Golden rays and azure bright,
Whisper secrets in the light.

Clouds dance softly, drifting slow,
Crimson whispers in twilight's glow.
Emerald dreams on sapphire streams,
Nature's art in vivid themes.

The sun dips low, a fiery ball,
Casting shadows, answering the call.
Each color sings a different tune,
A symphony beneath the moon.

In the evening, stars appear,
Winking gently, drawing near.
With every twinkle, every spark,
The night unveils its secret art.

A chorus of colors high and wide,
Each shade tells a story, side by side.
A fleeting moment, a timeless frame,
In the heavens, we'll speak their name.

## Light's Caress in the Silence

In the stillness of the night,
A gentle glow begins to ignite.
Moonbeams whisper, soft and clear,
Leading dreams that linger near.

Shadows stretch, then intertwine,
Wrapped in warmth, they softly shine.
Every corner holds a spark,
Lighting pathways in the dark.

Time flows slowly, hearts align,
In this moment, all is divine.
Light's caress upon the skin,
A tender touch that pulls within.

Silence sings a soothing song,
Inviting us where we belong.
In the quiet, truth unfolds,
With every breath, the night enfolds.

Lost in thought, we chance to find,
Fragments of the world entwined.
In the silence, light does dance,
With every heartbeat, every glance.

## Fragments of the Divine Palette

A brush of gold, a stroke of blue,
Each color tells a tale so true.
In this realm of painted dreams,
Inspiration flows in glowing streams.

Red like passion, fierce and bright,
A reminder of the love in sight.
Green whispers life, a gentle song,
In every shade, we all belong.

Textures mingling, layers deep,
Secrets of the heart to keep.
With every hue, a story blooms,
Echoing through forgotten rooms.

This palette speaks of worlds unknown,
In vivid shades, the seeds are sown.
From darkest nights to morning's grace,
Fragments of beauty we embrace.

In the gallery of our minds,
A tapestry of life unwinds.
Each brushstroke, a memory's dance,
The divine canvas offers chance.

## **Chasing Shadows of the Cosmos**

In the vastness, stars align,
A cosmic dance, a tale divine.
Nebulas swirl in colors bright,
Chasing shadows, embracing light.

Galaxies spin, a spiral song,
Whispers of worlds where we belong.
In the silence, dreams take flight,
A journey guided by the night.

Planets twirl in endless grace,
Mapping trails through time and space.
Each celestial body tells a tale,
Of distant realms beyond the pale.

Chasing shadows, glimpses bold,
Secrets of the universe unfold.
In every twinkle, every spark,
We find ourselves within the dark.

With every breath, we reach above,
In the vastness, we feel love.
As we chase these shadows near,
The cosmos sings, we lend an ear.

## **Twilight's Embrace**

As daylight fades to gentle night,
The sky adorned in hues of light.
Whispers of dusk begin to sing,
In twilight's arms, the stars take wing.

A soft breeze weaves through the trees,
Carrying secrets on the knees.
Shadows mingle, dreams unfold,
In twilight's warmth, the world feels bold.

Colors dance on the horizon's edge,
Nature clings to a silent pledge.
Each moment fleeting, but so divine,
In twilight's embrace, our hearts entwine.

A canvas painted with fading rays,
Where memories linger in soft arrays.
The day departs, but hope remains,
In twilight's glow, love sustains.

So let us linger in this phase,
In the stillness, our spirits praise.
For as the night begins to bloom,
Twilight's embrace dispels the gloom.

## Dancers of the Polar Sky

In the hush of the Arctic night,
Colors swirl, a vibrant sight.
Dancers twirl in the frozen air,
The polar sky, a master fair.

Ribbons bright on velvet dark,
Nature plays its timeless lark.
Swaying light in cosmic flight,
A dreamscape born of starry might.

With each flicker, a whispered sigh,
Echoes soft as they drift by.
In the stillness, magic stirs,
As the universe gently purrs.

Boundless beauty overhead,
A celebration where spirits tread.
Cold air crisp, hearts alive,
In this dance, the night will thrive.

We gaze up, our souls alight,
Beneath the wonder of the night.
Dancers weave through cosmic threads,
In the embrace where silence spreads.

## **Illuminated Reverie**

Beneath the moon's soft, silver gaze,
Whispers drift through evening's haze.
Dreams awaken in the tender light,
An illuminated, wondrous sight.

Stars align in a cosmic play,
Guiding thoughts that drift and sway.
In shadows cast by gentle glow,
Memories bloom, like flowers grow.

Eyes closed tight, we lose our way,
In reverie where the heart will stay.
Each moment cherished, softly spun,
As day departs and dreams begun.

Thoughts emerge like fireflies bright,
Twinkling whispers in the night.
Each glow a story waiting there,
In the silence, we breathe the air.

Awake in dreams, our spirits soar,
In this realm, forever more.
Illuminated by night's embrace,
Find solace in this sacred space.

## **Silver Streaks Across the Night**

In midnight's cloak, a soft surprise,
Silver streaks ignite the skies.
Comets racing through the dark,
While stardust leaves its fleeting mark.

Whispers travel on the breeze,
Through quiet woods and ancient trees.
Each flash a promise, a wish on high,
Silver trails that gently fly.

Night unfolds its sparkling cloak,
In the stillness, magic spoke.
Guided by their radiant flight,
We chase our dreams into the night.

Time stands still, as we unite,
Underneath the shimmering light.
Each moment a treasure to hold tight,
Silver streaks across the night.

And when dawn begins to break,
We'll remember dreams we dared to make.
With hearts aglow and spirits bright,
Chasing silver streaks into the light.

## Colors Born of Cosmic Fire

In the heart of the night so deep,
Blazing hues of secrets keep.
Crimson swirls in endless dance,
Ignite the dreams of midnight's glance.

Golden sparks like whispers flow,
Through the dark, they softly glow.
Azure trails paint the silent air,
A symphony of colors rare.

Emerald flames in a cosmic sea,
Cradle the light, wild and free.
Violet wisps where shadows bleed,
Awake the heart with every deed.

Radiant arcs in a stellar show,
Brush the heavens with cosmic flow.
In the silence, colors ignite,
Born of fire, a wondrous sight.

Each twinkle tells a story bright,
Of colors born in celestial light.
Through the void, they swirl and weave,
In cosmic fires, we believe.

# Celestial Ribbons in the Twilight Sky

As day bids farewell to the sight,
Twilight brings the stars to light.
Celestial ribbons twist and curl,
Weaving dreams in a twilight whirl.

Fading hues of amber grace,
Paint the edges of time and space.
Silent whispers of the night,
Glimmer and dance in the fading light.

Beneath the arch of the endless blue,
Twinkling lights begin to bloom.
Each ribbon sways in cosmic delight,
Embracing the twilight, soft and bright.

Crimson streaks and sapphire gleam,
Weave through the air like a whispered dream.
Holding secrets of the universe wide,
In their embrace, we find our guide.

Lost in the tapestry of stars,
Mapping the dreams of who we are.
In twilight's hush, our spirits fly,
On celestial ribbons across the sky.

## **Elysian Veils of the Night**

Softly draped in velvet skies,
Elysian veils where magic lies.
Stars cascade like gentle rain,
Whispers of beauty, void of pain.

Moonlit paths on which we tread,
Guide our hearts where dreams are fed.
In twilight's embrace, we forever dwell,
Under the charm of night's sweet spell.

Misty shadows weave and entwine,
Guardians of secrets divine.
With every breath, the night unveils,
The laughter of space in soft, sweet trails.

Silken threads of silvered glow,
Kiss the earth with gentle flow.
Each breath taken in the night,
Transports us to that realm of light.

In the silence, peace ignites,
Elysian veils of starry nights.
Whispered dreams in the cool night air,
Remind us of magic everywhere.

## **The Silent Ballet of Stars**

In the heavens, a dance unfolds,
The silent ballet of stories untold.
Stars sway gently, graceful and bright,
In the stage of the vast, endless night.

Together in harmony, they shine,
Each flicker a note, divine.
They twirl and leap, a cosmic flow,
Leading our hearts where dreams may go.

With every glance at twinkling light,
We feel the rhythm of the night.
A symphony written in cosmic dust,
Revealing the wonder; it's a must.

As night deepens, the dance expands,
Guided by celestial hands.
In the silence, we find our place,
Entranced by the stars' embrace.

So let us dance in their soft glow,
With the silent ballet; let our souls grow.
For in the dark, where no light mars,
We find ourselves among the stars.

## **Whispers of Heaven's Canvas**

In twilight's embrace, the stars align,
Brushstrokes of dreams, in soft design.
A gentle sigh from the moonlit sea,
Whispers of heaven calling to me.

Clouds weave tales in silver and gold,
With every stroke, a secret told.
The night is alive with delicate grace,
In the canvas of sky, we find our place.

Colors dance in galactic flow,
Echoes of worlds in the twilight glow.
From distant shores, the silence speaks,
In every heart, the yearning peaks.

A symphony played on the strings of light,
Stars twinkle softly, a beautiful sight.
Each moment a treasure, a fleeting dream,
In whispers of heaven, we find our theme.

Beneath the vastness, we stand so small,
Yet in our spirits, we hear the call.
Connected by threads of the cosmic night,
In whispers of heaven, we feel the light.

## Shimmering Horizon in the Cold

Beyond the frost where the sun meets the sea,
A shimmering line, wild and free.
The horizon glows, a beacon bright,
In the cold embrace of the fading light.

Crystal stars blink in the icy air,
Stars seem to dance, without a care.
Fractured reflections in the snow,
A silent promise of warmth to show.

Eager dawn paints the sky in hues,
Lavender whispers, pinks, and blues.
With every moment, the chill dissolves,
Wrapping the world in warmth it evolves.

Mountains shimmer under morning's kiss,
A sacred stillness, a moment of bliss.
Beneath the ice, life stirs awake,
In the shimmering horizon, hearts won't break.

Each ray of light ignites the land,
In a frozen dream, hand in hand.
Together we stand, in the cold we hold,
A shimmering horizon, a story retold.

## Frostbitten Colors of the Night

In the stillness where shadows creep,
Frostbitten colors begin to leap.
Emerald greens and sapphire blues,
Chill and wonder blend in the hues.

Moonlight shimmers on the icy ground,
Painting secrets, silent and profound.
The night enfolds, a woven cloak,
In every breath, the mysteries spoke.

Hints of gold in the darkest space,
Frosty glitters in a wild embrace.
The canvas whispers under starlit skies,
A dance of colors that mystifies.

Every twinkle tells a tale,
Of frosty nights and winter's veil.
In the heart of cold, the colors thrive,
Frostbitten dreams, forever alive.

Wrapped in warmth, we chase the night,
In a world of wonder, pure delight.
Together we find the beauty in sight,
In frostbitten colors, our hearts take flight.

## Arctic Glow: A Cosmic Saga

In the heart of the Arctic, magic unfolds,
A cosmic saga in twilight told.
With every flake that falls from the sky,
A dance of enchantment that draws the eye.

Colors collide in a radiant blaze,
Night's gentle touch sets the world ablaze.
Auroras flicker, green and red,
A celestial story by silence fed.

Whispers of ages in every beam,
The universe sings in graphite dream.
A palette of wonder paints the night,
In this Arctic glow, everything feels right.

Stars align in the frozen air,
A tapestry woven with utmost care.
Each glimmer a hope, a reason to soar,
In the cosmic saga, we explore.

Boundless and bright, the heavens call,
In the grandeur above, we feel so small.
Yet with every heartbeat, we come alive,
In the Arctic glow, our spirits thrive.

## Whispering Aurora

In the stillness of the night,
Colors dance across the sky,
Whispers of the stars ignite,
As the silent moments fly.

Gentle hues of green and gold,
Cradle dreams that softly gleam,
Tales of wonder yet untold,
Bathe the world in starlit beam.

Rippling through the icy air,
Nature's brush paints joy anew,
Lost in awe, we stand and stare,
While the cosmos whispers true.

Frozen breath and hearts ablaze,
Together in this mystic sight,
Time suspends in endless ways,
As the earth greets the nightlight.

Underneath the vast expanse,
We find solace in the glow,
In this celestial romance,
Hope and wonder freely flow.

## **Shimmering Nightfall**

As twilight drapes the world in grace,
The shadows play a gentle song,
Stars emerge in velvet space,
Whispering where we belong.

Moonlight weaves its silver thread,
Through the trees, it softly glows,
While the world now feels so led,
Into dreams where magic flows.

Glistening on the hidden stream,
Reflections dance like fleeting sighs,
In this moment, all can dream,
Beneath the vast and watchful skies.

Night's embrace, a velvet cloak,
Wraps the earth in calm delight,
In each breath, pure hope awoke,
Guiding hearts to rest tonight.

With each star, a story glows,
Of the secrets nightfall knows,
Shimmering in endless flow,
As we wander where time slows.

## Secrets of the Borealis

In the northern sky's soft sigh,
Colors bright in merry chase,
Borealis whispers from on high,
Shrouding dreams in a mystic lace.

Dancing lights in cosmic flight,
Embrace the earth in their delight,
Echoes of the cosmos' might,
Reveal the secrets of the night.

Every shimmer tells a tale,
Of ancient stars and ageless lore,
In the silence, we set sail,
To explore what came before.

With each stroke of light's caress,
Hearts entwined with nature's glow,
Finding peace in the finesse,
Of the world below and so.

These moments hold a sacred key,
Unlocking hopes in the divine,
In the dance of mystery,
We find where our spirits shine.

**Ethereal Dreams Unfurled**

In the twilight's gentle hold,
Whispers drift on the cool breeze,
Stories of the brave and bold,
Floating softly through the trees.

Colors merge in a soft blend,
As the sky begins to fade,
Time dissolves, and dreams descend,
In this magic, fears evade.

Celestial notes fill the air,
Lifting hearts with every chord,
In this dusk, no room for care,
As we sail on dreams restored.

Every flicker here reveals,
Hidden paths that we can trace,
Guided by the love that heals,
In the night's ethereal grace.

In this realm where shadows play,
We find solace, pure and bright,
Leaving behind the light of day,
Caught in dreams, we take our flight.

## Twilight's Brush

As day gives way to night,
The sky dons her softest hue.
Stars awaken, taking flight,
Whispering secrets old and new.

The breeze carries a gentle sigh,
While shadows dance upon the ground.
Echoes of a lullaby,
In twilight's grace, peace is found.

Crickets chirp a soft refrain,
Moonlight paints the world aglow.
Nature sings through joy and pain,
In the silence, dreams bestow.

A canvas brushed with dreams untold,
As night unfolds its mystic hand.
In the twilight's embrace, we're bold,
Together, we forever stand.

**Aurora's Serenade**

Dancing lights in the crisp night air,
Whispers of magic, bright and rare.
The horizon blushes, a vibrant show,
As night surrenders to the glow.

Colors swirl in a cosmic ballet,
Nature's art in a splendid display.
Stars twinkle softly, a guiding light,
Leading us through the enchanting night.

Each moment feels like a sweet embrace,
While shadows awaken, losing their trace.
In the dawn's gentle, tender kiss,
We find a world, a sparkling bliss.

Awake, the earth greets the day anew,
Under the skies, painted bold and blue.
Aurora sings in a timeless rhyme,
A serenade that transcends time.

## Embrace of the Sky

A canvas vast, the sky's expanse,
Clouds drift softly, lost in a trance.
Sunrise spills gold over land and sea,
In the embrace of the sky, we're free.

Birds take flight on a gentle breeze,
Life awakens among the trees.
Whispers of dreams in the morning light,
As shadows retreat from the flight.

Colors blend in a painter's hand,
Texture and hue from nature's grand.
With every heartbeat, we rise and sway,
Held by the sky in a sweet array.

As twilight falls, stars start to gleam,
The day whispers softly, "Dream, dream, dream."
In the embrace of the sky so wide,
We find our truth, our hearts abide.

# **Choreography of Colors**

A dance unfolds in shades so bright,
Crimson and gold in the morning light.
Every petal, every leaf,
Whispers stories beyond belief.

Brush of the wind, gentle and sweet,
Nature's rhythm beneath our feet.
Brushstrokes of emerald, sapphire, and flame,
In this vibrant world, all feels the same.

Like paint on a palette, splashes of hue,
Twirling and spinning, life feels anew.
A choreography that nature writes,
In the dance of day, in the heart of nights.

Watch the sunset, a grand finale,
As colors intertwine in a vibrant rally.
With every dusk, a song unfolds,
In this dance of colors, we find treasures untold.

# Flickers in the Arctic Sky

In the chill of polar night,
Stars begin their dazzling flight.
Whispers of the cosmic dance,
Call us to a mystic trance.

Colors blend, a vivid spray,
Painted skies in grand display.
Northern lights, they weave and twine,
Nature's brush, so pure, divine.

Gentle winds, they softly sigh,
Underneath the vast, dark sky.
Flickers pulse, a heartbeat's song,
In this realm where dreams belong.

Frosted breath, the world stands still,
Magic weaves through every hill.
Time is lost in twilight's kiss,
A moment wrapped in gentle bliss.

Serenity beneath the glow,
In the night, we come to know.
Every beam a story told,
In the Arctic, fierce and bold.

## **Luminescence Unbound**

In the dark, a spark ignites,
Dancing shadows take their flights.
Waves of light through midnight's veil,
Whispers sweet, a beckoning tale.

Crystals shine like scattered dreams,
Reflecting all the starlit beams.
Every pulse a heartbeat's grace,
In this vast and sacred space.

Mountains cradle light's embrace,
While the world finds its true place.
Every moment hangs in time,
As we rise through silent rhyme.

Nature's glow casts shadows deep,
As slumbering spirits start to leap.
Fields aglow with silver mist,
In this realm, we can't resist.

Journey forth through night's delight,
Embraced by dreams of soft twilight.
Luminescent paths unwind,
In the heart, there's peace to find.

## Enchantment of the Frost

Frosty breath upon the air,
Whispers of a world so rare.
Nature's blanket, soft and white,
Cradles secrets in the night.

Branches clad in crystal lace,
Glistening in their frozen grace.
Every flake, a story spun,
Kissed by warmth of winter sun.

Footsteps echo, soft and light,
In a land of pure delight.
Frosty patterns paint the ground,
Where enchantments can be found.

Glistening waves of chilly breeze,
Rustle softly through the trees.
Underneath the silver glow,
Promises of love will flow.

Enchantment fills the quiet night,
Stars twinkling, shining bright.
In this world of frost and gleam,
We awaken and we dream.

## **Waltz of the Winter Glow**

Join the dance of purest light,
As the world turns soft and white.
Snowflakes twirl through chilled air,
Weaving magic everywhere.

Glistening like gems above,
Nature sings of peace and love.
Every step in rhythm flows,
In the beauty that winter shows.

Whirling through the serene night,
Stars and frost in pure delight.
Twilight's breath, a gentle guide,
In this waltz, we do abide.

Underneath the moonlit beam,
Wondrous whispers, soft as dream.
Harvesting the calm we seek,
As the frosty peaks do speak.

Let the winter hold you tight,
As you bask in this soft light.
Waltz beneath the endless sky,
In this realm where souls fly high.

## The Light Beyond

In shadows deep, a spark ignites,
A flicker dances, hope alights.
Whispers of dawn, a hush bestowed,
Through darkest nights, the path is showed.

With every breath, the spirits rise,
A symphony of gentle sighs.
In every heart, a beacon shines,
Uniting souls, fate intertwines.

Beyond the veil, the truth awaits,
A world unfolds, unbarred gates.
In currents warm, our dreams take flight,
Together we embrace the light.

Through trials faced, we find our way,
In unity, we forge the day.
A tapestry of love is spun,
In every heart, we are as one.

So hold my hand, step forth with me,
In realms of hope, our spirits free.
For in the light that knows no end,
We find our truths, we transcend.

## **Tidal Waves of Glow**

Upon the shore, where oceans kiss,
A glow emerges, a tranquil bliss.
Waves of silver, tides that flow,
Carrying whispers, the night's soft glow.

In moonlit dance, reflections gleam,
A symphony of a lover's dream.
With every crest, the heart's embrace,
A melody time cannot erase.

From depths below, the pulses rise,
In harmony with starlit skies.
Each surge a tale, each crash a sound,
In tides of love, we are unbound.

As dusk retreats and dawn breaks free,
Nature's canvas, a vivid spree.
Embrace the ebb, surrender whole,
In tidal waves, we find our soul.

Together we stand, hand in hand,
Upon this shore, our hearts expand.
In waves of glow, forever sway,
In love's embrace, we'll find our way.

## Aurora's Caress

In velvet skies, a dance unfolds,
With colors bright, the night molds.
Auroras paint the darkened veil,
In whispers soft, the stars exhale.

A tapestry of light above,
A silent song, a tale of love.
With every shimmer, hearts ignite,
In aurora's arms, we find our flight.

As night gives way, the dawn will break,
A gentle touch, the earth will wake.
In shades of pink, in hues of blue,
The magic lingers, pure and true.

In nature's breath, we feel her grace,
In every ripple, a warm embrace.
Each moment bright, with wonder's bliss,
In aurora's glow, we find our kiss.

So let us wander, hand in hand,
In this embrace, we make our stand.
For in each flare, love's story grows,
In aurora's caress, our spirit flows.

## **Bistre Dreams**

In bistre hues, soft shadows play,
The world transformed at end of day.
Ink and warmth in twilight's breath,
A canvas rich, where dreams find depth.

With whispers low, the night concedes,
In quiet corners, our heart's needs.
A gentle sigh, a moment's pause,
In bistre dreams, love finds its cause.

The flicker dims, yet eyes still gleam,
In every glance, we dare to dream.
With every shadow, a story spun,
In hues of dusk, we become one.

Through night's embrace, our souls entwined,
In bistre night's warmth, a fate aligned.
With every heartbeat, love will bloom,
In richer tones, dispelling gloom.

So stay awhile, 'neath starlit streams,
And let us wander through these dreams.
For in this night, our hearts ignite,
In bistre dreams, we'll take our flight.

## Ghostly Flames in the Arctic Embrace

Whispers of frost in the night air,
Dancing lights, a silent prayer.
Shadows move in the icy still,
Nature's magic, a stunning thrill.

Beneath the stars, they weave and sway,
Cascades of colors on display.
Crimson and green, a fiery song,
In this embrace, we all belong.

The cold bites, yet spirits rise,
Glimmers twinkling in endless skies.
Frozen dreams that brightly gleam,
Ghostly flames in a midnight dream.

Cloaked in twilight, the world stands still,
Illuminated by the heart's will.
In frigid realms, a love so bright,
Guided by these stunning lights.

An arctic glow, serene and bold,
Patterns of stories yet untold.
Together, we chase the light's embrace,
In the ghostly flames, we find our place.

## **Melodies of a Starlit Sky**

Softly hums the night so deep,
While the stars around us leap.
Whispers of cosmos fill the air,
With each twinkle, a tale to share.

Underneath this vast expanse,
Time slows down; we breathe, we dance.
Celestial notes on gentle winds,
As the universe softly spins.

Glistening orbs, so far, so bright,
Guide our dreams through the still night.
From dusk till dawn, the stories flow,
In harmonies only we know.

A symphony crafted of hope and light,
Bathed in the glow of cosmic flight.
Each star a chord, each planet a sound,
In this galaxy, love is found.

Melodies drift in the cool night breeze,
Whispered dreams in the rustling leaves.
Together we breathe this stellar sigh,
Under the deep, starlit sky.

## Dreaming in Electric Hues

In a world of neon dreams,
Colors burst at the seams.
Electric lights on whispered streets,
Rhythm and pulse, where heartbeats meet.

Dancing shadows, vibrant and bold,
Moments captured, stories told.
Every hue holds a voice within,
In vivid landscapes, we begin.

Sparks ignite in the midnight air,
Colors twirl with the utmost care.
In every shadow, a memory glows,
As twilight drapes in liquid flows.

Through the maze of shimmered delight,
Chasing dreams into the night.
In this canvas of electric bliss,
We find the magic we don't want to miss.

With every heartbeat, colors bloom,
Painting life in the darkest room.
Dreaming wide in a world askew,
Awash in shades of electric hue.

## **Nature's Secret Lightshow**

In the forest, shadows play,
Crickets sing to end the day.
Between the trees, soft glimmers peek,
Nature's whispers soon to speak.

Fireflies dance with gentle grace,
Lighting paths in this sacred space.
Flickering lights in harmony's tune,
Beneath the watchful, silver moon.

Rustling leaves with secrets told,
Every shimmer, a dream unfold.
In the twilight, magic stirs,
Nature's beauty, all that occurs.

Colors blink in this vast embrace,
Mysterious beings in hidden place.
A secret show from land to sky,
Awakening wonder, as time slips by.

In silence, we join the night's refrain,
Captivated by this soft, sweet gain.
Nature's light show, both wild and free,
A radiant gift for you and me.

## Cosmos in Motion

Stars dance softly, glowing bright,
Galaxies swirl in the velvet night.
Planets whisper tales untold,
In the vastness, dreams unfold.

Nebulas bloom in colors rare,
Nebulous wonders float in air.
Comets race with fiery trails,
Charting paths where silence prevails.

Time is but a fleeting spark,
Eternity's essence in the dark.
Black holes beckon, mystery calls,
As cosmic wonder gently falls.

Constellations weave ancient lore,
Guiding sailors to distant shore.
In the heavens, secrets gleam,
Filling our hearts with astral dreams.

Cosmic tides ebb and flow,
Carrying us where starlight glows.
Together we drift in this grand expanse,
Lost in the universe's endless dance.

## Serene Auroras

Under skies of emerald grace,
Dancing lights in a tranquil space.
Whispers of the northern breeze,
Gentle sway of ancient trees.

Colors blend in a wondrous show,
Illuminating all below.
Nature's brush paints night divine,
A tranquil canvas, soft and fine.

Majestic waves of violet glide,
Merging where the shadows hide.
In a silence, hearts will sway,
As the auroras dance and play.

Celestial colors weave and spin,
Each moment a new tale begins.
In this magic, time stands still,
As dreams awaken, hearts will fill.

Gazing upward, souls align,
In the light, we intertwine.
Where serenity finds its way,
In the auroras' soft display.

## Echoes of the Chill

Cold winds whisper through the night,
A serenade of fading light.
Frost-kissed leaves in crisp embrace,
Echoing winter's silent grace.

Shadows stretch in twilight's hold,
Stories of the night unfold.
Footsteps crunch on frozen ground,
In this stillness, peace is found.

Moonlight dances on the snow,
Guiding where the lovers go.
Stars above like diamonds bright,
Illuminate the quiet night.

Time slows down, the world feels small,
Wrapped in winter's cozy call.
Echoes linger, soft and clear,
In the chill, there's nothing to fear.

As dawn creeps in, the chill will fade,
Leaving whispers of dreams made.
In its wake, warmth will fill,
Echoes of the evening chill.

## **Twinkling Serenity**

Stars ignite the velvet sea,
Whispers of serenity.
Each twinkle tells a gentle tale,
Carried softly by the gale.

Moonlit paths on tranquil lakes,
Where the heart and spirit wakes.
Reflections dance in silver light,
Guiding souls through the night.

Time slows in the evening glow,
As the world begins to slow.
Gentle sighs in the midnight air,
Wraps us in a tender care.

In stillness, dreams begin to form,
Hush of night, a soothing warm.
Amidst the stars, a silent plea,
For endless peace and harmony.

Twinkling sky above our heads,
Gifts of beauty softly spread.
In this moment, let us be,
Lost in twinkling serenity.

# Ethereal Glow of the Night

Stars whisper secrets of old,
In a tapestry of silver and gold.
The moon hangs low, a watchful eye,
As dreams take flight, like clouds in the sky.

Silken shadows dance on the ground,
In this quiet world, peace is found.
Night wraps its arms, a gentle embrace,
While time slows down in this sacred space.

Each breath draws in the stillness around,
In the nighttime's heart, magic is found.
The world fades away, just you and the light,
In the ethereal glow, everything feels right.

Glimmers of starlight weave through the trees,
A soft, gentle hum carried by the breeze.
The horizon blushes as darkness unfolds,
A canvas of wonder, a story retold.

In the quiet, let your spirit roam,
Discover the beauty, make the night home.
Ethereal glow, a guiding spark,
Leading our souls through the depths of the dark.

## **Luminous Brushstrokes on Darkness**

With each stroke, the cosmos ignites,
Painting the sky with dazzling lights.
Colors collide in a vibrant embrace,
While shadows retreat, finding their place.

A canvas of night, brushed with delight,
Whispers of colors connect the light.
Crimson and cobalt, a radiant show,
In the depths of the night, brilliance will flow.

The artist's hand dances, wild and free,
Crafting a vision for all eyes to see.
Luminous tendrils of gold and of blue,
Wrap the horizon in a radiant hue.

Each star a promise, a wish to fulfill,
In this painted realm, hearts never stand still.
The darkness gives way to this vibrant hue,
As dreams take shape, as hopes shine anew.

Luminous brushstrokes ignite the night,
Transforming the canvas with relentless might.
In this dance of color, let your heart soar,
Embrace the magic, forever explore.

## **Chasing the Painted Sky**

With every brush of dawn's golden ray,
The dreams of night slowly melt away.
Chasing colors that dance on the breeze,
Through the open fields, under whispering trees.

As day breaks free, the world comes alive,
Nature awakens, its colors arrive.
Pastels and golds spill across the scene,
In a masterpiece where hopes intervene.

Chasing the hues as they shift and blend,
A fiery promise that never will end.
Each moment a canvas, a story to tell,
In the painted sky where our spirits dwell.

With laughter and joy, hearts race like the sun,
In this vibrant chase, we are all one.
Chasing the painted horizon ahead,
Letting the colors weave dreams in our heads.

The sky unfolds like a tale on the run,
A limitless journey, the adventure begun.
Chasing the painted sky, let us aspire,
To dance through the colors, to sparkle like fire.

## **Celestial Streams of Color**

In the twilight, a river of stars,
Flows through the night with wonders from afar.
Celestial streams in a cosmic embrace,
Whispering tales of time and of space.

Colors cascade like a gentle song,
Weaving through shadows where dreams belong.
With each hue, a secret is told,
In a luminous stream where the heart feels bold.

From indigo depths to hues soft and bright,
Every bend sparkles, each turn ignites.
Celestial pathways where stardust roams,
In this endless river, our spirit finds homes.

Brushstrokes of velvet coat the night sky,
In an infinite dance, we're invited to fly.
Celestial streams where imagination flows,
Connecting our souls in the light that glows.

With wonder as our guide, we'll follow the light,
Through celestial rivers, we'll soar to new heights.
In this colorful journey, let freedom unfold,
In celestial streams of color, brave and bold.

## Prism Between Worlds

In fields where shadows blend with light,
Colors swirl in endless flight.
A prism bends the rays we see,
Unveiling realms that long to be.

Each hue a dream, each shade a sigh,
Whispered tales of earth and sky.
Between the worlds, we wander free,
Where heart and soul find harmony.

The morning dew, like jewels cast,
Reflects the echoes of the past.
A prism's arc, a bridge, a key,
Unlocks the depths of mystery.

With every step, the dance unfolds,
In twilight's grasp, our fate beholds.
In light's embrace, we find our way,
Through vibrant dreams that forever stay.

So let us chase what lies ahead,
In colors bright, no tears to shed.
A realm of wonder waits for us,
In prisms bright, we place our trust.

## **Celestial Echoes**

Stars above in velvet night,
Whisper softly, pure delight.
In moonlit trails, the echoes play,
Guiding hearts along the way.

Galaxies spin, a cosmic dance,
Inviting minds to take a chance.
Our wishes drift on stardust streams,
While time unfolds in silken dreams.

Constellations tell our tale,
In stories heard on softest gale.
The cosmic clock, it ticks so slow,
As secrets of the heavens flow.

A quiet hum, celestial sound,
Resonates in hearts unbound.
With every twinkle, hope ignites,
In endless realms of starry nights.

So gaze above and let it be,
In silence feel the mystery.
The universe, a grand ballet,
In celestial echoes, we shall stay.

## Secrets of the Arctic Night

Whispers weave through frozen air,
Underneath the moon's soft glare.
Winds of mystery softly sigh,
In Arctic realms where dreams can fly.

A blanket white on silence lies,
As midnight paints the starlit skies.
In shadows deep, the secrets keep,
Where ancient hopes and lost souls sleep.

Glistening ice, a mirror's truth,
Reflects the wisdom of our youth.
In frozen echoes, stories blend,
Of journeys taken, paths that wend.

Northern lights like breath of fate,
Dance above the world's cold gate.
They weave our dreams in shades of green,
On canvas vast, serene, unseen.

Beneath the stars, the heartbeats blend,
In stillness, find what nature sends.
The Arctic night, a sacred space,
Where secrets thrive, a warm embrace.

## Shimmering Veil of Dusk

As daylight fades, the colors blend,
A shimmering veil begins to send.
The sunset bleeds in shades of gold,
Wrapping the world in warmth untold.

A moment paused, the sky ignites,
With whispers soft of starry nights.
In dusky hues, the dreams take flight,
Entwined in shadows, pure delight.

The horizon whispers secrets rare,
In twilight's grasp, we find our prayer.
Each stroke of dusk, a painter's touch,
A world transformed, it means so much.

As night descends, the stars align,
The universe begins to shine.
With every breath, the calm unfolds,
In shimmering veil, our heart beholds.

So sit with me where shadows play,
And let the night wipe tears away.
In dusk's embrace, we softly sway,
Forever lost, we find our way.

## Cosmic Embers of Winter

In the chill of the night, stars gleam bright,
Snowflakes dance softly, a pure delight.
Wind whispers secrets, a soft, gentle sigh,
Under the blanket of a deep, dark sky.

Crimson and silver paint the frozen land,
Footsteps echo lightly, a moment so grand.
Trees stand tall, draped in glistening white,
A cosmic embrace in the shimmering light.

Fireplaces flicker, casting warmth around,
Voices intermingle, a comforting sound.
In this tranquil space, time loses its grip,
While we share our dreams with each whispered slip.

Frost-kissed horizons stretch far and wide,
Endless horizons where mysteries bide.
Under the cosmos, we dance in our hearts,
Together we weave, for winter imparts.

Embers of starlight guide us tonight,
Through the whispers of long, tender night.
In the silence we find our peace so rare,
Under the spell of snowflakes in the air.

**Subtle Hues in Frozen Air**

A quiet dawn breaks, colors soft and pale,
Shimmers of blue in the frosted veil.
Breezes carry whispers of nature's embrace,
In the gentle morning, we find our place.

The world is painted in soft, tender light,
Hues of pastel whisper, a delicate sight.
Footprints leave stories on the glistening ground,
In the silence of winter, our hearts are unbound.

Amber sunbeams stretch across the field,
Revealing the beauty that the frost has sealed.
Trees adorned with crystals, a brilliant display,
Reflecting the wonders of a brand new day.

As shadows grow long, the chill finds its mark,
Yet warmth fills the air, igniting a spark.
Life breaths in colors that gently unfold,
In the art of the winter, secrets are told.

Within this frozen pause, we find our calm,
Nature's rich tapestry, a soothing balm.
Subtle hues linger, in every cold breath,
A reminder of warmth, even in death.

# Nocturnal Symphony of Colors

The night unfurls with a magical tune,
Dancing lights shimmer beneath the moon.
Stars play a melody, a cosmic affair,
In the darkened sky, colors twist and flare.

With each twinkling note, dreams start to weave,
Whispers of longing, a place to believe.
Shadows embrace where secrets reside,
In the nocturnal symphony, magic won't hide.

Crickets strum harmonies, soft, yet so sly,
While lanterns of fireflies flicker and fly.
The cool night air carries laughter and cheer,
In this canvas of life, everything is near.

Reflecting in rivers, the stars find their path,
Colors converge, igniting our wrath.
Underneath the vastness, we sigh and stare,
In this infinite beauty, we find our share.

As dusk greets the dawn, the colors will blend,
Nocturnal symphony slowly meets its end.
Yet in our hearts, the echoes will stay,
A reminder of night, as it fades into day.

# **Radiant Secrets Beneath the Stars**

Under the velvet sky, secrets reside,
In the rustle of leaves, where dreams softly glide.
Stars shimmer brightly, each a tale untold,
In their radiant glow, our stories unfold.

Night blossoms gently, painted in light,
Whispers of magic fill the still night.
With each passing moment, we delve deep within,
Discovering treasures beneath our skin.

Cosmic lullabies cradle us tight,
While fireflies flit in the soft moonlight.
The pulse of the universe beats in our chest,
In this dance of creation, we find our rest.

Galaxies twirl, lost in the vast,
Every heartbeat echoes, a connection amassed.
In the quiet of night, we learn to embrace,
The radiant secrets of time and space.

As dawn approaches, colors start to blend,
But the whispers of night will never quite end.
In the heart of the cosmos, forever we'll be,
Entwined in the magic of eternity.

**Frosty Tendrils of the Night Sky**

In whispers deep, the night unfolds,
Stars whisper secrets, ages old.
A silver veil, the frost does weave,
On every breath, the night does grieve.

Moonlight dances on a frozen lake,
Shadows shimmer, the silence wakes.
Tendrils curl in a chilling embrace,
Nature's breath leaves a haunting trace.

Beneath the vast, eternal stretch,
Time stands still, a silent sketch.
Each twinkle tells a tale untold,
Of dreams once dreamt, now long grown cold.

The wind carries a lullaby's tune,
Guiding lost souls to the moon.
Through the frost, a journey unfolds,
In the heart of night, magic holds.

Glistening whispers, the night air sighs,
As frost creeps forth, the old world dies.
Yet in the shadows, hope's not shy,
For dawn will break on the frosty sky.

## **Ethereal Dreams in Arctic Air**

In a realm where silence reigns,
Ethereal visions break the chains.
Whispers of snow on the icy ground,
Dreams drift softly, veiled and bound.

The auroras dance with gentle grace,
Colors merge in an endless chase.
Through the chill, a spark ignites,
Elysian realms in the fading lights.

Every breath forms a crystal lace,
In this land, time loses pace.
Echoes of the past linger near,
In frozen air, memories sear.

With each dawn, a soft embrace,
Nature's beauty leaves its trace.
In the silence, hearts take flight,
Chasing dreams in the Arctic night.

The horizon blushes with morning hue,
Painting the frost with tears anew.
In this realm of dreams laid bare,
Ethereal whispers fill the air.

## Light's Journey Through the Void

In the void where shadows dwell,
Light emerges, casting a spell.
With each flicker, a cosmic dance,
In the silence, it takes its chance.

Stars ignite in a vast expanse,
Chasing fate in a timeless trance.
Through the dark in vibrant threads,
Woven tales, where silence spreads.

Light's path bends and twists with grace,
Guiding wanderers through endless space.
In that void, a promise glows,
A beacon where hope gently flows.

Moments flicker, and time takes flight,
In the heart of the endless night.
From nothingness, a spark will bloom,
Banishing echoes of deepening gloom.

So follow light through the abyss,
An eternal dance, an endless kiss.
In the void's embrace, dreams connect,
A journey vast that we'll protect.

## Celestial Fireflies in the Dark

In the velvet shroud of the night,
Fireflies burst with gentle light.
Flickering dreams like whispers call,
In the dark, they rise and fall.

A dance of stars in a silent sea,
Their glow, a map for hearts set free.
Each ember glints with a tale to tell,
As shadows weave in a magic spell.

Through the dusk, they wander far,
Guided softly by each small star.
A luminous path where wishes glide,
Celestial guides on a moonlit ride.

Crickets sing in the evening fine,
While fireflies blink in rhythmic line.
Nature's chorus swells and flows,
As night reveals the light that grows.

In the darkened world, a spark ignites,
Celestial fireflies, the night's delights.
With every flicker, they cast their cheer,
A testament to love's frontier.

# **Nightly Kaleidoscope**

Stars scatter wide like dreams so bright,
   Colors swirl softly in the night.
A dance of shadows and radiant light,
   Whispers of magic take their flight.

Moonbeams weave through the velvet skies,
   Illuminating secrets, where wonder lies.
The world beneath stirs, gently sighs,
   In the embrace of the night's soft ties.

Crickets serenade, their songs so sweet,
   Echoes of laughter in every heartbeat.
Nature's symphony, a harmonious feat,
   In this kaleidoscope, all souls meet.

Glimmers of hope in every glance,
   Eyes full of wonder, a celestial dance.
Lost in the moment, in a timeless trance,
   Under the stars, our hearts advance.

Night's canvas painted with colors bold,
   Stories of old in whispers told.
In this nightly show, we behold,
   A tapestry rich, a sight to mold.

# **Wonders of the Celestial Sphere**

Upon the canvas of dark and deep,
Planets twirl in their endless sweep.
Galaxies spiral, secrets to keep,
In the universe's embrace, we leap.

Comets blaze trails of fleeting light,
Passages written in the quiet night.
Tales of time travel, a wondrous sight,
In the celestial dance, hearts take flight.

Constellations whisper tales of old,
Myths interwoven, stories told.
In the heavens' arms, we behold,
A shimmering path of dreams and gold.

Nebulas swirl in colors divine,
The cosmos pulses with a vibrant sign.
A celestial body, forever to shine,
In the vast expanse, our spirits align.

Through telescopes aimed and dreams so high,
Humanity gazes at the endless sky.
In wonder and awe, we still can fly,
In the celestial sphere, we learn to dream why.

## Flickering Auras

In the twilight glow, soft lights dance,
Flickering auras, a fleeting glance.
Colors merge in a mystical trance,
Nature's brush in a radiant romance.

Whispers of winds tell tales anew,
Beneath the stars, in the night's soft hue.
Visions shimmer in a spectral view,
Awakening the magic in me and you.

From the fireflies that light the dark,
To the moonlit streams, where dreams embark.
Every flicker, a joyful spark,
In the canvas of night, we make our mark.

Auras of hope in the shadows creep,
Embracing the lull, where secrets sleep.
In the quiet night, our hearts leap,
In the flickering light, memories we keep.

So let us wander where the night is fair,
Where the flickering auras fill the air.
In this luminous glow, emotions lay bare,
Guided by dreams, we dance without care.

## Luminous Tales

In the night's embrace, stories ignite,
Luminous tales in the fading light.
Each star a whisper, a spark of delight,
Guiding our hearts through the velvety night.

Moonlight casts shadows, a gentle glow,
Illuminating paths where wanderers go.
Every flicker, a tale we know,
In the quiet night where wonders flow.

Winds carry secrets, soft and true,
Rustling leaves share tales with you.
In every corner of the sky so blue,
Journeys unfold in the night's debut.

A tapestry woven with dreams and care,
Every luminous tale, a moment rare.
With every glance, we are drawn to share,
The magic that lingers, a bond to declare.

So come take a step into the unknown,
Where luminous tales in the night are sown.
In the heart of darkness, our spirits have grown,
In the glow of the night, we find our home.

## **Celestial Glimmers**

In the silence of the night,
Stars whisper tales of light,
Each shimmer holds a dream,
In the cosmos, we all gleam.

Planets dance in gentle sway,
Galaxies unfold their play,
Nebulae in hues profound,
Wonders in the dark abound.

Comets trace their fleeting arc,
Lighting up the endless dark,
A cosmic ballet in the skies,
Infinite secrets in their rise.

Moonbeams weave a silver thread,
Kissing softly as we tread,
On the path of starlit gleam,
Guiding us through every dream.

Heaven's canvas stretches wide,
Embracing hope, a timeless guide,
In celestial glimmers bright,
We find solace in the night.

## **Dreams Adrift in Stardust**

Floating soft on cosmic seas,
Wandering with the gentle breeze,
Dreams adrift in stardust light,
Painting shadows of the night.

Galactic whispers fill the air,
Echoes reach us from somewhere,
Hopes entwined in twinkling rays,
Guiding hearts through endless days.

Black holes hold their secrets tight,
Yet in darkness, we find light,
Each dream an atom of the whole,
Binding stories to the soul.

Supernovae burst and bloom,
Filling the vast, eternal room,
In their aftermath, we find,
Life's adventures intertwined.

Sailing through this endless night,
Wrapped in dreams, we find our flight,
As stardust shapes our hopes anew,
In the cosmos, we break through.

## **Glittering Horizons**

At dawn's first blush, horizons gleam,
Whispers rise from a waking dream,
Colors spill in radiant hues,
A canvas with endless views.

Mountains touch the sky so high,
Grasping stars as they pass by,
Rivers flow like silver threads,
Running where the heart treads.

Waves crash on the sandy shore,
Echoes chant the tales of yore,
Every sparkle in the sea,
Holds a secret meant for me.

With every breath of morning's light,
Hope ignites, burning bright,
Embracing all that lies ahead,
On glittering horizons, we're led.

Chasing sunsets, catching dreams,
In every shimmer, magic gleams,
The horizon calls us near,
In every heartbeat, we appear.

## Frosted Luminosity

In winter's chill, a glow appears,
Frosty whispers greet our ears,
Crystals dance on branches bare,
Painting sparkles in the air.

Moonlight bathes the snowy ground,
Silent beauty all around,
Each flake tells a tale so rare,
Of frosted dreams that linger there.

The night sky dons a silvery robe,
Framing realms we seldom probe,
Gentle light in endless flow,
Illuminates the world below.

Stars twinkle with a frosted sheen,
In this magic, we're serene,
Boundless wonder we embrace,
In the quiet, we find grace.

Wrapped in warmth, we share the glow,
Stories told in whispers low,
Frosted luminosity's kiss,
Brings a world of frozen bliss.

## Mysteries of the Frosted Sky

Whispers fly on winter's breath,
Beneath the frost, dreams hide in death.
A shimmer calls through the pale night,
Where secrets dance in silver light.

Stars shiver in their timeless glow,
Veiled in snow, they seem to know.
Echoes of the past entwine
With shadows cast, a silent sign.

The moon hangs low, a watchful eye,
Tracing paths where memories lie.
In every flake, a story spun,
Each frozen tear, a tale begun.

Night's canvas, brushed with ice and fear,
Holds the laughter of those near.
In the quiet, hearts collide,
Finding warmth where dreams reside.

Mysteries linger, wrapped in night,
Frosted sky glows with hidden light.
Reach up high, let the wonder soar,
In the silence, seek forever more.

## The Glow Beneath Stars

In the hush of twilight's grace,
Glow ignites in a tender place.
Beneath the stars, the world expands,
A shimmering dance in our hands.

Crickets sing their evening tunes,
As fireflies waltz beneath the moons.
Soft breezes carry scented dreams,
In the glow, reality gleams.

Whispers echo through the night,
Crafting magic in pure delight.
Every twinkle tells a tale,
Of journeys traveled without fail.

Hands entwined, we roam so free,
In the glow, just you and me.
Stars above, our guiding light,
In this moment, hearts ignite.

Veils of darkness may surround,
Yet the glow is always found.
Underneath the vast expanse,
Love emerges in the dance.

Together we shall always shine,
Beneath the stars, our lives align.
With every heartbeat, we explore,
The glow of love forevermore.

## Dance of the Midnight Veil

Underneath the shroud of night,
Veils of mystery take to flight.
Whirling softly in the dark,
Each flicker holds a hidden spark.

Time stands still as shadows play,
In the nocturne's soft ballet.
Winds of twilight weave and twirl,
Embracing dreams in a silent whirl.

Echoes linger, breaths align,
In a dance, eternally entwined.
Stars peep through the midnight mist,
Every moment a lover's tryst.

Twilight drapes in silken threads,
Where beauty flows and longing spreads.
Under the moon's alluring gaze,
We find ourselves in a timeless haze.

Hold me close as we unfold,
In this veil, our stories told.
With every rhythm, hearts conspire,
In the night, we spark the fire.

So dance with me through endless night,
Wrapped in dreams, we chase the light.
Where every shadow blooms anew,
The midnight veil belongs to you.

## Enchanted Skies

In the canvas of the night,
Colors spark, a wondrous sight.
Dreams unfurl in vibrant hues,
Beneath the skies, we seek the clues.

Whispers of the stars above,
Sing the ancient tales of love.
Each constellation, a guide so true,
Leading hearts to start anew.

Clouds drift softly, tales untold,
Carrying secrets of the bold.
As the horizon meets the dawn,
A new adventure, we are drawn.

Together we'll uncover the skies,
In the magic where the heart lies.
Every twinkle, a wish we make,
In enchanted realms, we will awake.

Let the wonders cast their spell,
In the ethereal, all is well.
As we gaze, our spirits fly,
Embraced in the enchanted sky.

## Snowy Radiance

Blankets of white cover the ground,
Whispers of silence all around.
Sparkling crystals dance in the light,
Nature's beauty, a pure delight.

Trees wear coats of glistening frost,
In this stillness, no moment is lost.
Footprints lead through a winter's dream,
Under the glow of the moon's beam.

Snowflakes twirl like delicate lace,
Each unique in its quiet grace.
A world transformed, serene and bright,
Wrapped in the warmth of snowy night.

Children laugh as they sled and play,
Creating memories in winter's sway.
Joyful shouts echo through the air,
In this snowy wonder, nothing compares.

As the sun sets with a gentle sigh,
Colors fade in the evening sky.
Snowy radiance softly gleams,
In the heart of winter, we weave our dreams.

## **In the Arms of Aurora**

Dancing lights paint the evening sky,
As colors merge and swirl up high.
In whispers soft, the night unfolds,
Stories of magic in shades of gold.

Cascading ribbons of emerald green,
Flowing like water, a mesmerizing scene.
Each flicker tells tales of old,
In the arms of aurora, mysteries hold.

Night creatures stir from their serene pause,
Awed by the beauty, they take a cause.
Nature's canvas, alive with fair,
In every heartbeat, enchantment shares.

As dawn approaches, the colors fade,
Yet the memories linger that evening made.
In this embrace, I find my place,
In the arms of aurora, I slow my pace.

Dreams linger on in morning's light,
Echoes of wonder take their flight.
With every sunrise, love stays near,
In the arms of aurora, my heart is clear.

**The Skies' Secret Symphony**


Above the world, a melody flows,
Written in clouds where the soft wind blows.
Each note a whisper, a gentle sigh,
The skies compose their song on high.

Stars join in with a twinkling sound,
In cosmic rhythm, they spin around.
Galaxies weave in a dazzling dance,
As constellations take their chance.

The moon reflects in silvery threads,
Guiding the night through dreams it spreads.
A lullaby sung by the evening's breath,
The symphony plays until the dawn's depth.

With every heartbeat, the music grows,
In harmony where the starlight glows.
Nature listens, cradled and still,
In the skies' secret, hearts feel the thrill.

As morning breaks, the notes retreat,
Yet in our souls, the echoes greet.
Forever cherished in memory's embrace,
The skies' secret symphony leaves its trace.

## **Celestial Threads**

Woven in darkness, the stars display,
Threads of starlight guiding the way.
Each glimmer a story, bold and bright,
In the tapestry of the cosmic night.

Nebulas bloom like flowers unseen,
Colors collide in a vibrant sheen.
Through the infinite, dreams softly glide,
In celestial threads, our hopes abide.

Planets spin in their rhythmic grace,
Orbiting sunlight with tender embrace.
Cosmos dances in perpetual stride,
In every heartbeat, the universe bides.

With every glance at the endless sky,
We feel a connection that never says goodbye.
The threads of existence, tightly knit,
Binding all beings in infinite wit.

As whispers of night surrender to day,
The celestial threads still hold their sway.
In every heartbeat, a world we've spun,
Under celestial threads, we're forever one.

## Veils of Twilight

Shadows stretch on whispering ground,
A dance of dusk without a sound.
Stars begin their silent plea,
As night unfolds its mystery.

A gentle breeze calls softly near,
Caressing dreams, dissolving fear.
The world transforms, a dusky hue,
Where secrets hide and spirits brew.

Moonlit paths weave through the trees,
Guiding souls with tender ease.
In twilight's arms, we sway and roam,
Finding solace, we are home.

Glimmers peek through fading light,
Painting the sky with silver bright.
Each star a wish, a whispered hope,
In twilight's grasp, we learn to cope.

Embrace the night, let shadows play,
In veils of twilight, dreams hold sway.
As dawn approaches, we find our way,
Renewed in heart for a new day.

## **Ethereal Glimmer**

In the still of night, stars align,
A soft glow emerges, divine.
Crystals dance on dewy grass,
Whispers of magic that softly pass.

The moon casts pearls upon the sea,
Each wave a note in harmony.
Chasing shadows that twinkle bright,
Infusing dreams with celestial light.

A flicker of hope in a darkened hour,
Nature's grace, a gentle power.
As fireflies waltz in the warmest air,
Their brilliance woven, a treasure rare.

Through the stillness, a heartbeat hums,
Echoes of life as the universe thrum.
In this glow, we find our core,
An ethereal vision we can't ignore.

Embrace the glimmer that sparks the night,
A beacon of joy, a promise bright.
With every twinkle, find your place,
In the vastness of time and space.

## **Celestial Ballet**

Stars pirouette in the velvet sky,
With comets trailing, they drift by.
Nebulas swirl in colors bold,
Tales of the cosmos quietly told.

The planets spin in their ancient waltz,
In rhythmic patterns, they never halt.
Each movement crafted with care and grace,
Together they form an endless space.

Galaxies bloom like flowers bright,
Painting the canvas of endless night.
Twinkling dancers in a cosmic jest,
Filling the universe, they never rest.

In silence, the orbits weave and twine,
Creating a symphony, fluid and fine.
With each heartbeat of the celestial ball,
We are but specks, yet within it all.

Join the dance as the stardust calls,
In the vast expanse, our spirit soars.
With every step in this ethereal realm,
We find our truth at the cosmic helm.

## **Gleaming Tapestry**

Threads of gold and silver shine,
Woven stories in every line.
Each pattern whispers tales of old,
Embroidered dreams in hues of gold.

Underneath the sun's warm embrace,
Life's colors blend in a sacred space.
Every stitch holds a memory dear,
A tapestry spun from laughter and tears.

In shadows cast, the fibers sway,
Creating shadows where hopes may play.
Fingers dance on a loom of chance,
Weaving futures in a vibrant trance.

Celebrate the beauty, bright and vast,
In this woven world, memories cast.
From every thread, a story we gain,
A gleaming tapestry of joy and pain.

Embrace the fabric of life we share,
Each moment cherished, forever rare.
In every weave, a piece of heart,
Together we create a work of art.

## **Enigma of the Frozen Glow**

In twilight's hush, the snowflakes fall,
Whispers of secrets in silence call.
Glistening shards of a forgotten fate,
Wrap the world in a silver spate.

A lantern shines with a ghostly light,
Guiding lost souls through the endless night.
Patterns of frost on the windowpane,
Sketch tales of joy mixed with ancient pain.

Beneath the stars, shadows softly creep,
Guardians of dreams that the night will keep.
Echoes of laughter in winter's embrace,
Cradle the warmth of a bygone place.

Mysteries dance in the winter's breath,
Life intertwined with the specter of death.
In this realm, where the past holds sway,
Time flickers like candles, fading away.

A frozen glow wraps the heart in wonder,
As night unveils its mystical thunder.
Finding solace in the chilling breeze,
The enigma whispers, it's time to seize.

**Chroma of the Arctic Night**

Colors emerge in the cloak of night,
Painting the sky with a dazzling light.
Auroras weave through the icy blue,
A canvas alive with a vibrant hue.

The stars awaken, soft and bright,
Illuminating paths with their gentle light.
Each shimmer holds a story untold,
Of ancient wonders and dreams of old.

Whispers of wind carry tales unseen,
Of lands uncharted and what has been.
Through frozen forests, shadows deeply roam,
Guiding the wanderers, far from home.

In this embrace of the starry dawn,
The heart feels light, as fears are gone.
With every heartbeat, a promise ignites,
To dance in the colors of Arctic nights.

A tapestry woven with threads of frost,
In the colors of dusk, we find what's lost.
Let the night cradle your wandering soul,
In the chroma's embrace, we become whole.

## Celestial Threads in the Frigid Air

Silent threads of the cosmos descend,
Weaving dreams that the stars commend.
Each twinkle a hope, a whispering prayer,
Floating softly through the frigid air.

Frozen lace in the moon's sweet glow,
Cascading light in a tranquil flow.
Wonders awaken with the night's embrace,
Embroidered whispers in this sacred space.

Time stands still as the heavens align,
Guiding the lost through the dark, divine.
Moments entwined like the finest silk,
A tapestry rich as the purest milk.

Glimmers of fate in the icy expanse,
Holding hands with chance in a cosmic dance.
The heart feels the pull of the starry thread,
In the canvas of night, all courage is fed.

As we breathe in the chill of the hour,
The celestial weave unveils its power.
In the depths of winter's chilling glare,
We find our place in the frigid air.

## Dance of the Celestial Spirits

In twilight's glow, the spirits convene,
Dancing in shadows, elusive and keen.
With laughter and sighs, they twirl and sway,
Under the gaze of the moon's soft ray.

Veils of mist, they twine and weave,
As stars in the heavens quietly breathe.
Gentle whispers echo through the night,
Inviting all souls to share in their flight.

The frosted trees play a timeless tune,
While starlight winks from the watchful moon.
Chasing the echoes of laughter's song,
In the dance of the spirits, we all belong.

Colors blend as the night unfolds,
Revealing the mysteries that silence holds.
Each movement a story, a life once known,
In the cosmic ballet that feels like home.

With every flicker, the night comes alive,
A celebration of spirits that forever thrive.
In this celestial dance, we find our part,
As the universe mingles with the mortal heart.

## **Radiant Silence**

In the stillness, whispers sigh,
Stars above, like dreams, float high.
Moonlight bathes the world in grace,
Peaceful heart, in soft embrace.

Gentle night wraps all in shade,
Moments linger, never fade.
Crickets play their soothing song,
In this silence, we belong.

Veils of dusk, a calming hue,
Nature's blush, a vibrant view.
Each breath taken, soft and light,
Carried on the wings of night.

Time stands still, the world at rest,
In the quiet, feel the best.
Inner thoughts, like rivers flow,
In this silence, let love grow.

Radiance shines from every heart,
In the depths, we find our part.
Together woven, threads divine,
In this moment, pure, you'll shine.

## **Waking the Heavens**

With golden dawn, the skies ignite,
Birds awaken, taking flight.
Softly breaking, night's embrace,
Morning's kiss, a sweetened grace.

Colors burst, a vibrant show,
As the world begins to glow.
Gentle breezes, whispers stir,
Nature hums with life's own purr.

Mountains greet the sun's first rays,
Fields of blooms, in vibrant plays.
Each petal dances, fresh and bright,
In this glory, pure delight.

Clouds like brushstrokes grace the air,
A canvas painted with such care.
As the heavens slowly wake,
Life anew, each moment take.

Through the day, the joy cascades,
Heart to heart, in sunlight wades.
Every heartbeat resonates,
Waking love that never waits.

## **Enigmatic Radiance**

In shadows deep, a light appears,
Mystery glows, banishing fears.
Silent echoes, soft and clear,
In this radiance, draw near.

Stars conspire in the night,
Secrets whispered, pure delight.
Every shimmer, stories told,
In the dark, their warmth unfolds.

Glimmers dance on silver streams,
Weaving through forgotten dreams.
Lost in thought, a gentle sigh,
Truth unveiled; no need to lie.

Navigating through the haze,
Finding beauty in the maze.
Every moment, holding tight,
In the enigma, find your light.

In the stillness, courage grows,
Through the quiet, wisdom flows.
Embrace the radiant, the rare,
In every heartbeat, love lays bare.

## **Dancers in the Sky**

As twilight falls, the stars align,
Cosmic rhythm, grand design.
Planets twirl in a cosmic spree,
Dancers weaving, wild and free.

Comets blaze their fleeting trails,
Celestial songs on whispered gales.
In the dark, each spark ignites,
Guiding dreams on starry nights.

When the moon takes its proud throne,
Shadows stretch, yet we're not alone.
Gathered round this astral show,
Life's abundance starts to flow.

Galaxies spin in endless grace,
Within the vast, we find our place.
Connected hearts in cosmic dance,
In this silence, take a chance.

So look above, and you will see,
The universe, in harmony.
Together, we are bound and tied,
As dancers in the sky, we glide.

## **Aurora's Elusive Embrace**

Whispers dance on frosty air,
Shadows play without a care.
Colors swirl in silent flight,
A dream unfolds in the night.

Light unfolds in curtains bright,
Painting darkness with pure light.
Nature's brush, a tender trace,
Capturing Aurora's grace.

Moonbeams weave through chilly skies,
As the world begins to rise.
With each flicker, hearts ablaze,
In the magic, we are lost in praise.

Glittering stars in endless space,
Reflect the dance we all embrace.
In this moment, love ignites,
In Aurora's wings of vibrant flights.

Wrapped in hues of green and gold,
Stories of eternity unfold.
Elusive whispers in the breeze,
An embrace that leaves us at ease.

## Colorful Tales of the Arctic Night

Under whispers of the pines,
A canvas full of secret signs.
Crimson glows and sapphire gleams,
We bask within our frozen dreams.

Icicles hang like crystal chains,
Nature's artwork, beauty reigns.
Whimsical tales in shadows spun,
Under the watchful northern sun.

Polar bears in quiet grace,
Drift through snow in a slow embrace.
Auroras whisper ancient lore,
Of the night and what's in store.

Waves of silence fill the air,
Hearts connect in night's warm glare.
Mysteries in every flake,
Colorful tales the night will make.

As stars twinkle in a frosty sky,
We gather 'round with hopeful sighs.
In Arctic's embrace, we hear the call,
Together beneath the moonlit hall.

# **Revelry of the Cosmic Soirée**

In the depths of starry skies,
Galaxies swirl like painted eyes.
Whirling through the vast unknown,
Invitations to realms unshown.

Comets plunge with dazzling grace,
Lighting paths in time and space.
Cosmic melodies resonate,
Echoing fates that intertwine and wait.

Spinning orbs in harmony,
Unfolding tales of mystery.
Nebulas in vibrant bloom,
A dance of colors in the gloom.

Together, we share this grand delight,
Hearts ablaze in the velvet night.
With every glance and every twirl,
Stars align, making magic whirl.

As the universe sways and dips,
We savor moments, silk and slips.
In this endless cosmic show,
We find ourselves, the starlight's glow.

## Starlit Hymn of an Endless Sky

Above the hills, the stars ignite,
Singing softly, pure delight.
Whispers travel on the breeze,
Boundless tales amid the trees.

Each twinkle holds a story told,
Of nights forgotten, dreams of old.
Celestial music, a gentle sigh,
Awakens secrets from the sky.

In the vastness, we stand still,
Hearts entwined with every thrill.
Galaxies echo as we chase,
The starlit hymn in time and space.

Through the darkness, our hopes climb,
In this moment, we transcend time.
Constellations guide our way,
As dreams in silence gently sway.

Let the cosmos be our guide,
In beauty's arms, forever tied.
In endless sky, our souls unite,
Singing softly through the night.

## Canvas of Stardust

In the night sky, whispers gleam,
Stars are like dreams, woven in stream.
Each twinkle tells a story of old,
A tapestry of wonders, waiting to unfold.

Beneath the vastness, hearts collide,
With every flicker, secrets confide.
Galaxies dance in a cosmic play,
Painting the night, chasing shadows away.

Winds of time carry echoes afar,
While wishes float, a universal star.
The canvas deepens in midnight blue,
Where mysteries linger, waiting for you.

Moments captured in spectral light,
Glimmers of hope in the silent night.
With every heart, a piece of the sky,
Together we dream, together we fly.

In this stardust, we find our place,
Tracing the paths of every face.
The universe breathes in every sigh,
In the canvas of stardust, we will never die.

## Aether's Embrace

In warm embrace of twilight hue,
The world transforms, wild and new.
Aether sings a soft refrain,
Whispers carried on the gentle rain.

Clouds drift softly, dreams take flight,
In the cradle of the fading light.
Stars awaken, twinkle divine,
As shadows dance on the ancient vine.

With each heartbeat, the night unfolds,
Stories linger, quietly told.
Ethereal visions in the cool breeze,
Whisper secrets among the trees.

Embrace the silence, find your peace,
In twilight's arms, all worries cease.
Aether wraps us in calm delight,
As every soul finds solace tonight.

From dusk till dawn, a love will grow,
In the gentle touch of the afterglow.
Bound by the whispers of the sky,
In aether's embrace, we learn to fly.

## **Frosted Glow**

Morning breaks, the world aglow,
A frosted blanket, a sparkling show.
Crystals glisten on every bough,
    Nature's art, a sacred vow.

Each breath taken, clouds of white,
Shimmering flakes in the soft daylight.
The sun emerges, warm and bright,
    Kissing the frost, a joyful sight.

In the stillness, whispers blend,
Chill in the air, winter's friend.
Footprints crunch on the icy path,
Tracing the art of nature's wrath.

Glistening rivers flow with grace,
Reflecting light in a frozen embrace.
Time stands still, as wonders grow,
In the heart of winter's frosted glow.

As shadows stretch, dusk will weave,
A tranquil charm we won't believe.
Wrapped in beauty, we'll find our flow,
    In the magic of the frosted glow.

## Translucent Reverie

In dreams, we wander, soft as light,
A translucent realm, wondrous and bright.
Clouds of shimmer, whispers of air,
Softly beckon, we drift without care.

Through fragile visions, we glide and sway,
Each fleeting thought, a dance in play.
In colors fading, hopes gently spin,
A reverie of echoes, where dreams begin.

Patterns unfurl in the twilight's grace,
Illuminating our hidden space.
With open hearts, we trace the way,
Through realms of wonder, come what may.

In the stillness, reflections bloom,
A luminescent dance in the twilight's room.
Embraced by shadows, we lose our fight,
In a translucent reverie, pure and light.

Every heartbeat pulses, a gentle sigh,
As we hold the universe, just you and I.
In dreams we linger, forever free,
In the realm of translucent reverie.

# Fractals of the Firmament

Stars whisper softly in the night,
Each twinkle a tale of ancient light.
Galaxies dance in a cosmic waltz,
Unraveling secrets within the vaults.

Nebulas bloom in colors bold,
Painted tales of the universe told.
Infinite patterns in dark embrace,
Fractals of wonder in endless space.

Time stretches thin as we gaze above,
Lost in the mysteries stars speak of.
A woven tapestry, vast and free,
The firmament's secrets, a sight to see.

Comets trace paths like dreams that flow,
Eclipses whisper of tales from below.
Each constellation a story spun,
A journey begun where the night is won.

Beneath this dome, we ponder our place,
In fractals of heaven, our souls we trace.
Forever seeking, we yearn to know,
In the firmament's arms, our hearts will grow.

## **Luminous Brushstrokes**

A canvas stretched across the sky,
Where sun and moon's embrace draws nigh.
Brushstrokes of color in twilight's blend,
Nature's palette, a sight to commend.

Golden hues kiss the horizon soon,
With splashes of pink beneath the moon.
Sapphire waves crash upon the shores,
Creating art that forever soars.

Dancing lights twinkle, stars ignite,
Crafting wonders in the veil of night.
Whispers of colors on canvas bright,
Luminous visions that fill with delight.

Chasing shadows, the painter's delight,
Merging the day with the soft, dark night.
Every sunset a brushstroke unique,
In the sky's gallery, peace we seek.

From the strokes of dawn to dusk's deep sigh,
Artistry blooms as moments fly.
Each day a masterpiece painted bold,
Luminous brushstrokes, a story told.

## Night's Dazzling Cloak

Underneath night's dazzling cloak,
Whispers of dreams begin to provoke.
Stars like jewels, they shimmer bright,
Guiding our thoughts through the silent night.

In the stillness, secrets unfold,
Stories of love, both timid and bold.
Moonlight weaves with shadows entwined,
A dance of time where hearts are aligned.

The breeze carries laughter, soft and sweet,
As echoes of night bring solace and heat.
Each moment wrapped in velvet embrace,
Night's cloak shrouds us in tranquil grace.

Mysteries linger, a sweet serenade,
In the glow of the night, we are not afraid.
For within this cloak, dreams take flight,
And life reveals its enchanted light.

Eclipsing the worries of the day,
Under the stars, we find our way.
In night's dazzling cloak, we feel so alive,
Together in dreams, where we thrive.

# **Spectrum of the Frozen Expanse**

In the frozen expanse where silence reigns,
Shimmers reflect in crystalline chains.
A spectrum vibrant beneath the cold,
Nature's wonders and mysteries unfold.

Icicles hang like delicate art,
Each one etched with a winter's heart.
Colors gleam in the bright sunlight,
Transforming frost into pure delight.

Winds whisper secrets through branches bare,
Echoes of magic cling to the air.
Snowflakes dance upon the chilly ground,
A symphony soft, a haunting sound.

Mountains stand tall in their regal might,
Guardians of dreams in the pale moonlight.
The frozen canvas, serene and stark,
A spectrum of beauty in every arc.

As dawn breaks forth, colors ignite,
Wrapping the world in warmth, pure and bright.
In the frozen expanse, we find our peace,
Nature's embrace, a sweet release.

## **Chasing Celestial Hues**

In twilight's grasp, the colors swirl,
With dreams aloft, our hearts unfurl.
We chase the stars, each glint and gleam,
In cosmic light, we dare to dream.

The orange blaze, the violet shade,
In fleeting moments, memories made.
Horizons stretch as shadows blend,
In chasing hues, our souls ascend.

Beneath the vast and endless dome,
We find our way, we feel at home.
A symphony of light and fire,
Each passing hue, our hearts inspire.

The stardust trails, the echoes sing,
Of ancient tales and future's wing.
We carve our paths, both bold and bright,
In chasing hues, we find our light.

## **Aurora's Whisper**

In the quiet night, the auroras play,
With ribbons of light that softly sway.
They dance and twirl in the frosty breeze,
A whispered song that puts hearts at ease.

Across the sky, a canvas aglow,
With emerald flames, they ebb and flow.
Each flicker tells of stories untold,
In nature's grace, we find the bold.

Caught in the magic, we gaze in awe,
As night reveals its wondrous law.
In silence, the cosmos draws near,
With every streak, we shed our fear.

A fleeting glimpse of the world's embrace,
In aurora's arms, we find our place.
Each whisper of light, a gentle kiss,
In nature's heart, we find our bliss.

## Dance of the Glistening Skies

When dusk arrives, the skies ignite,
With diamonds scattered, pure and bright.
The heavens twist, a waltz of hue,
In fleeting moments, we find what's true.

With each new star, the stories wake,
In cosmic light, we find our stake.
The glistening paths, the trails of gold,
In dance of skies, new tales unfold.

As twilight's veil begins to fall,
We hear the universe's call.
With every twinkle, a promise shines,
A whispered truth that intertwines.

In the night's embrace, our spirits soar,
In dance of skies, we crave for more.
Every glance upward, a heart's delight,
In glistening skies, we chase the night.

## Radiance Above the Pines

The sun ascends in golden grace,
Casting warmth on nature's face.
Among the pines, its light will weave,
A tapestry that we believe.

In morning's glow, shadows retreat,
As beams of hope begin to meet.
Each dewdrop glistens, a jeweled prize,
In nature's arms, we realize.

With every rustle, the forest sighs,
In harmony, the world complies.
Radiance spills like liquid gold,
In silence shared, our stories told.

Among the trees, we find our way,
In sunlit paths, we long to stay.
With pines as witnesses, we roam,
In radiance bright, we find our home.

## **Shimmering Ice Crystals**

In the stillness of the night,
Ice crystals catch the light.
Each one a fleeting dream,
Dancing in a silver beam.

Fractals twirl in icy lace,
Nature's art, a frozen grace.
Whispers of the winter's chill,
Magic in the air, so still.

A glistening ground beneath my feet,
Where silence and the coldness meet.
Colors shift from blue to white,
As the stars ignite the night.

Time stands still in frozen air,
Moments captured, crystal rare.
With every breath, the world seems bright,
In the glow of winter's light.

One by one, the crystals fall,
Nature's frigid, wondrous call.
In their beauty, secrets lie,
Beneath the sprawling, endless sky.

## **Twilight's Embrace**

The sun dips low, a gentle sigh,
Painting hues across the sky.
Shadows stretch in soft retreat,
As day and night begin to meet.

Whispers float in dusky air,
Secrets shared without a care.
Silhouettes in twilight glow,
As stars awaken one by one.

The moon peeks out, a silver crest,
In twilight's arms, the world finds rest.
A tranquil silence, time suspended,
In this moment, all is blended.

Colors blend, a painter's stroke,
In this light, all worries cloak.
Each heartbeat finds a soothing pace,
Wrapped within twilight's embrace.

Dreams take flight in night's embrace,
Hopes set free, they find their place.
Underneath the starlit dome,
In twilight's arms, we feel at home.

# The Eloquent Canopy

Beneath the trees, the whispers weave,
Tales of time that they believe.
Leaves murmur in the softest breeze,
Nature's voice among the trees.

A tapestry of greens unfurls,
With every branch, the magic swirls.
Dappled sunlight sifts through high,
Painting shadows as birds fly.

Within this world, the echoes roam,
Each heartbeat finds its way back home.
Roots entwined in soil's embrace,
Life's dance in a sacred space.

Ancient wisdom in bark and leaf,
Life's cycles hold both beauty and grief.
Beneath the canopy's watchful gaze,
We wander through nature's maze.

In every rustle, a story speaks,
In every branch, adventure seeks.
The eloquence of nature's hue,
Fills our hearts with wonder anew.

## **Frozen Prism**

In the frosty morning light,
Nature wears a crown so bright.
Prisms dance on snowy trails,
Echoing the beauty that prevails.

Icicles hang like crystal spears,
Glistening gems throughout the years.
Winter's breath upon the ground,
Creates a world so profoundly sound.

In every sparkle, joy resides,
As the silent snowflakes glide.
Each one unique, a fleeting grace,
In this tranquil, frozen place.

Colors shift with every glance,
Nature's hues in a frosted dance.
With every step, a soft, new song,
In frozen realms where dreams belong.

The sunlight breaks, a gentle tease,
Turning ice to shimmering ease.
In the heart of winter's prism,
Life reflects a timeless rhythm.

# Ethereal Nightfall

Stars shimmer like silver threads,
The moon bathes the world in grace.
Soft shadows dance on the ground,
Whispers of dreams interlace.

A cool breeze weaves through the trees,
Carrying secrets from afar.
Night creatures sing their gentle tunes,
Beneath the watchful evening star.

Velvet skies envelop the earth,
In a warm embrace of night.
Each moment drifts like a leaf,
Floating softly in pure delight.

The world unwinds in tender hush,
As colors fade into the dark.
Ethereal visions glide by,
Leaving behind a glowing spark.

In this tranquil, sacred space,
Time feels like a sweet refrain.
With each heartbeat, life slows down,
As nightfall weaves its gentle chain.

## Reverberating Colors

Colors burst in vibrant bloom,
Painting dreams on canvas skies.
Each hue a song, each shade a tune,
Where imagination freely flies.

Golden rays of morning light,
Chase away the lingering night.
Emerald leaves and sapphire seas,
Dance to the tune of the gentle breeze.

Crimson sunsets spark the heart,
A masterpiece that time imparts.
With every dawn, new colors rise,
In an endless play, a sweet surprise.

As twilight fades, the world ignites,
In hues of purple and soft grays.
The whispering shadows invite us near,
To savor the quiet end of days.

In this vibrant, swirling dance,
Nature sings its bold refrain.
Reverberating through our souls,
Colors echo, love's sweet gain.

## Cascading Illumination

A river of light flows gently down,
Waves of glow that softly play.
Golden beams through branches crown,
Whispering tales of the day.

Like a waterfall in mid-spring rise,
Illumination pours with grace.
Unfolding beauty in every guise,
A luminous glow we embrace.

Fleeting moments caught in gold,
Memories glisten, bright and bold.
Each gleam a story wrapped in light,
Guiding us through the darkest night.

In the twilight, shadows stretch long,
Yet hope flickers, ever near.
Cascading light, a heart's sweet song,
Whispers of love in every sphere.

With each dawn, we rise anew,
Chasing the glow that never fades.
In this dance of light and hue,
We find our path as love cascades.

**Whispers of the Cosmos**

In the stillness, silence sings,
Echoes of stars in the night.
Cosmic tales on soft winds bring,
Wisdom wrapped in starlight bright.

Galaxies swirl in endless dreams,
Celestial bodies pulse and glow.
In this dance of cosmic beams,
The universe whispers secrets low.

Time flows gently in the vast,
A river of moments intertwined.
Each heartbeat a note from the past,
In the endless expanse of the mind.

Through cosmic paths, we find our way,
Guided by light, we dare to explore.
Whispers from the void gently sway,
Unlocking mysteries evermore.

As humanity reaches for the skies,
With wonder etched in every face.
We listen deep, where silence lies,
In whispers of the cosmos' embrace.

Milton Keynes UK
Ingram Content Group UK Ltd.
UKHW021045031224
452078UK00010B/588